GOOD N

DADS

WORDS OF WISDOM
AND INSPIRATION FOR DADS

COMPILED BY LISA KING

CROSSWAY BOOKS · WHEATON, ILLINOIS
A DIVISION OF GOOD NEWS PUBLISHERS

GOOD NEWS FOR DADS

Copyright © 1998 by Good News Publishers

Published by
CROSSWAY BOOKS
A division of Good News Publishers
1300 Crescent Street, Wheaton, Illinois 60187

First printing, 1998. Cover and book design: Cindy Kiple. Photos: Harry Cutting.
Printed in the United States of America.

ISBN 0-89107-995-5

06		05		04		03		02		01		00		99		98
15	14	13	12	11	10	9	8	7	6	5	4	3	2	1

ESPECIALLY FOR YOU

It is our desire that Good News for Dads *inspire and challenge you in your God-given role as a father. He has entrusted you with an awesome responsibility. We want to support you in that task.*

Through the promises of Scripture and the insights of godly men and women from the past and present, we trust that this book will empower you to fulfill God's call as a father. Our hope is that some kernel of truth or piece of wisdom you find in these pages will strengthen your spirit, encourage your heart, or challenge your mind. And in doing so that God will work through you to positively influence those who mean the most to you. ❖

Nothing in this life can bring a greater sense of joy

and fulfillment than your family.

KURT BRUNER

❖

A daddy is the guide and wagon scout for his

child on the trail through life.

FRANK MINIRTH

True greatness is expressed in serving, not dominating. ❖

GARY CHAPMAN

By wisdom a house is built,

and through understanding it is established;

through knowledge its rooms are filled with

rare and beautiful treasures.

PROVERBS 24:3-4

❖

There is no substitute for spending time with your

children—and when you are with them,

really be with them.

R. KENT HUGHES

❖

Being a dad is more than just a role.

It's a God-given mission. ❖

A N O N Y M O U S

The workshop of character is everyday life.

M A L T B I E   B A B C O C K

❖

A man of knowledge uses words with

restraint, and a man of understanding

is even-tempered.

PROVERBS 17 : 27

A father is a man who is always learning how to love. ❖

ADRIAN ROGERS

Children properly nurtured in a home become the

strengthening fiber in society.

T O N Y   E V A N S

As the father is followed, so must he follow the Father.

A dad not pressing ahead in his own spiritual life

cannot lead his family where it needs to go.

GREG   JOHNSON

❖

The righteous man leads a blameless life;

blessed are his children after him.

PROVERBS 20:7

❖

Be careful for nothing, prayerful for everything,

thankful for anything.

DWIGHT L. MOODY

It's not what your child thinks of you now that's as important as what he thinks of you twenty years from now. ❖

SUSAN ALEXANDER YATES

Nearly all that I know about God I learned first from my father. ❖

RAYMOND I. LINDQUIST

What we have heard and known, what our fathers

have told us, we will not hide them from their

children; we will tell the next generation the

praiseworthy deeds of the LORD, his power, and the

wonders he has done. . . . Then they would put their

trust in God and would not forget his deeds but

would keep his commands.

PSALM 78:3-4,7

❖

What matters most in life is not what ladders

we climb or what ownings we accumulate.

What matters most is a relationship.

MAX LUCADO

❖

When you feel you're at the end of your

rope, remind yourself whose hand is

holding the other end.

NANCY KENNEDY

❖

21

The Final Four, the World Series, the Super Bowl,

the Stanley Cup, and the NBA Finals are thrilling

highlights of every year. But they are nothing

compared to the excitement of a family

intent on living for God.

ROLF ZETTERSTEN

❖

Child-rearing is not a competitive sport.

ANONYMOUS

If any of you lacks wisdom, he should ask God, who gives generously to all without finding fault, and it will be given to him. ❖

JAMES 1 : 5

Kids catch awe—or apathy—from people they admire,

starting with their parents. If nothing moves us,

they will soon lose their awe for

God and his creation.

DANIEL R. VANDER ARK

We will give an account, to God, for our own

actions—not our children's reactions.

LEE EZELL

Too many families are conducted on the basis of "I love you until further notice." That might work for the lover, but it doesn't work for the lovee.

RON HUTCHCRAFT

I don't have much money or property to hand down

to my kids, but I do have me. And that's what

they're going to remember anyway.

BRAD LEWIS

We make our decisions; then our decisions

turn around and make us.

RAY PRITCHARD

❖

If the love of God for the human race

is as great as the love of parents for their children,

then it is truly great and ardent.

MARTIN LUTHER

❖

Authentic men aren't afraid to show affection,

release their feelings, hug their children, cry when

they're sad, admit it when they're wrong,

and ask for help when they need it.

CHARLES SWINDOLL

❖

It is not learning that makes a man holy and just, but a virtuous life makes him pleasing to God. ❖

THOMAS À KEMPIS

Few things will exasperate a child more than inconsistency. Pity the horse that has a rider who gives it mixed signals, digging his heels into its side and pulling the reins at the same time. Pity the child even more who has the rules changed by a capricious father, and who is always exasperated because of the conflicting messages he receives. ❖

R. KENT HUGHES

34

I've been staggered by the number of men and women across the country whose most positive memory of their father was this: "I saw him reading his Bible and heard him praying for me."

JOHN TRENT

❖

God gave us children as a

blessing, not a chore.

JANIS MEREDITH

❖

I long to accomplish a great and noble task, but it is my chief duty to accomplish humble tasks as though they were great and noble. The world is moved along, not only by the mighty shoves of its heroes, but also by the aggregate of the tiny pushes of each honest worker.

HELEN KELLER

A godly leader takes great care with his children, knowing they are his single greatest contribution to the world. ◆

RAY PRITCHARD

Love is patient, love is kind. It does not envy, it does not boast, it is not proud. It is not rude, it is not self-seeking, it is not easily angered, it keeps no record of wrongs. Love does not delight in evil but rejoices with the truth. It always protects, always trusts, always hopes, always perseveres.

1 CORINTHIANS 13:4-7

❖

Listening—not very expensive, but it's probably the

most valuable gift we'll ever give our children.

ELAINE MINAMIDE

❖

Help us, O Lord, when we want to do the right thing, but know not what it is. But help us most when we know perfectly well what we ought to do, and do not want to do it.

PETER MARSHALL

❖

Good parenting has a way of crossing generations

to inspire its children's children.

CALVIN   MILLER

❖

The LORD is righteous in all his ways and loving toward all he has made. The LORD is near to all who call on him, to all who call on him in truth. He fulfills the desires of those who fear him; he hears their cry and saves them. ❖

PSALM 145:17-19

When people insist on perfection or nothing, they get nothing. ◆

EDITH SCHAEFFER

The most effective parents are those who have the

skill to get behind the eyes of their child, seeing

what he sees, thinking what he thinks,

feeling what he feels.

JAMES DOBSON

❖

Encouragement is one of the most powerful gifts you

can give your children. It is a gift that nurtures

competence and confidence and optimism.

JANIS LONG HARRIS

❖

If our goal is to raise perfect kids, we need a reality check. If our goal is to be a perfect parent, we're going to fail at that, too! The good news is that if our children know they're loved—fiercely and passionately—we have a chance. ❖

KAREN SCALF LINAMEN

You are the children of the LORD your God. . . .

DEUTERONOMY 14:1A

❖

Why is it that we often give the most of our time to those who care about us the least, and the least of our time to those who care about us the most? We should prioritize everything on the basis of who will cry at our funeral.

PATRICK MORLEY

❖

If you want your children to honor you, you must live a life worthy of their honor. ◆

RAY PRITCHARD

Many fathers who would never harm their children

physically are discarding them emotionally

and spiritually by being silent in

their nurture and training.

TONY EVANS

❖

Sons are a heritage from the LORD,

children a reward from him.

*I'm glad the father of the Prodigal Son wasn't presented
as a failure, even though his son left home prematurely,
partied, and lost everything. Dad was the hero of
the story—a wise and caring parent. Judge your
parenting by the quality of your love for your
children, the role model you set before them, and the
appropriateness of your actions and reactions toward
them—not by what you aren't able to fix.*

BUDDY SCOTT

❖

I am the way and the truth and the life. No one

comes to the Father except through me.

JOHN 14 : 6

❖

To belittle is to be little.

ANONYMOUS

❖

The Bible tells us that where our treasure is, there our heart will be also. Time is a treasure. Where we invest our time, our heart will follow. ❖

KAREN SCALF LINAMEN

Know therefore that the LORD your God is God; he is the faithful God, keeping his covenant of love to a thousand generations of those who love him and keep his commands. ◆

DEUTERONOMY 7:9

Children are a lot like chickens . . . they need room

to squawk, lay a few eggs, flap their wings,

even to fly the coop.

CHARLES SWINDOLL

Effective parenting can be

summed up in one loaded sentence:

Look beyond your child's deeds to his needs.

RON HUTCHCRAFT

❖

To pray only when in peril is to use safety

belts only in heavy traffic.

CORRIE TEN BOOM

❖

Dads, we must ruthlessly refuse to let our sin collect

and contaminate our own and our loved ones' lives.

The great news for those who know Jesus Christ

is that we can live pure lives.

JOHN TRENT

❖

Mom and Dad were wise enough to broaden my knowledge of God beyond going to Sunday school, saying grace at dinner, and memorizing a lot of Bible verses. They understood that every dimension of our lives is indeed spiritual. ❖

JONI EARECKSON TADA

O LORD, our LORD, how majestic is your name in all the earth!

You have set your glory above the heavens. From the lips

of children and infants you have ordained praise. . . .

PSALM 8 : 1 , 2 A

❖

Don't pretend to your children that you're

perfect. They know you're not.

ADRIAN ROGERS

❖

[handwritten: 918 744/257]

[handwritten: 918 7440200]

There is no greater legacy for a man to leave than wisdom. ◆

HOWARD HENDRICKS

We would like to think that we can become

capable and effective fathers while avoiding the

work, pain, and process necessary. Instant

father *is an attractive myth.*

TIM HANSEL

❖

A Christian should be an alleluia

from head to foot.

ST. AUGUSTINE

❖

God is interested in your prayers because he is interested in you. . . . He's your Father; he wants to hear what you have to say. In fact, he's waiting for you to call. ❖

BILL HYBELS

Lavish affection on your children! Children can't be hugged and kissed too much by both mom and dad. Affection is the medium of acceptance. ◆

R. KENT HUGHES

God demonstrates his own love for us in this:

While we were still sinners, Christ died for us.

ROMANS 5 : 8

Large chunks of time aren't your only opportunities

to take pleasure in your children. Each day can be a

treasure chest full of magic moments.

JANIS MEREDITH

❖

Emotionally healthy kids live in an environment where parents attempt to catch them doing something right rather than something wrong—and where more energy is invested in praising children for being successful than criticizing them for falling short of expectations. ❖

H . N O R M A N   W R I G H T   A N D
G A R Y   J .   O L I V E R

The true character of a person is seen not in momentary heroics but in the thump-packed humdrum of day-to-day living. ◆

Give, and it will be given to you. A good measure,

pressed down, shaken together and running over,

will be poured into your lap. For with the measure

you use, it will be measured to you.

LUKE 6:38

❖

Humor diffuses stress in a family, pulls bricks out of the walls that come between us, and helps us remember why we liked each other in the first place. ❖

KAY BISHOP

God never got around to creating

a substitute for experience.

A D R I A N   R O G E R S

❖

Vulnerability fits beautifully into mature manhood. So does integrity. ❖

CHARLES SWINDOLL

A little active dependability proves much of

truthfulness, and truthfulness produces trust.

WALTER WANGERIN

❖

Priorities are a grid to help us distinguish

opportunity from distraction.

PATRICK MORLEY

❖

And you, my son Solomon, acknowledge the God of your father, and serve him with wholehearted devotion and with a willing mind, for the LORD searches every heart and understands every motive behind the thoughts. If you seek him, he will be found by you; but if you forsake him, he will reject you forever. ◆

1 CHRONICLES 28:9

Heredity does not equip a child with proper attitudes;

children learn what they are taught.

JAMES DOBSON

❖

Listening to a child is more than

the absence of talking.

RON HUTCHCRAFT

❖

For you have been my hope, O Sovereign LORD, my confidence since my youth. From birth I have relied on you; you brought me forth from my mother's womb. I will ever praise you. ❖

PSALM 71:5,6

The church is looking for better methods;

God is looking for better men.

EDWARD M. BOUNDS

❖

Our children copy everything we do. This is one of the most terrifying truths of parenthood.

RAY PRITCHARD

❖

Failing to build a strong relationship with your wife because you don't think you need one yourself is to deprive her of her need. The same thing goes for your children. ◆

TONY EVANS

Service to others is the highest

pinnacle man ever scales.

GARY CHAPMAN

❖

Children's children are a crown to the aged, and

parents are the pride of their children.

PROVERBS 17:6

❖

Long-distance fathering doesn't work. . . .
Letters and telephone calls do not build
relationships. ❖

PETER FELDNER

Children may be the little trumpet players who

bring us to our senses, and to our knees.

BILLY GRAHAM

❖

A man is someone who rejects passivity,

accepts responsibility, leads courageously,

and expects a greater reward.

ROBERT LEWIS

❖

Above all, love each other deeply,

because love covers over a

multitude of sins.

1 PETER 4:8

❖

Children are harmed more by our

apathy than our error.

JAY STRACK

❖

The child who has not been disciplined with love

by his little world will be disciplined, generally

without love, by the big world.

ZIG ZIGLAR

No man ever became great doing as he pleased.

❖

Very young children need to make eye contact with a parent every few minutes. This simple availability communicates to the child, "I'm here. You are special to me, and I will take care of you." It doesn't require much effort to turn away from the book we are reading, the TV program we are watching, or the work we are doing and connect with the child. ❖

JAMES MALLORY, M.D

Christianity is the highest perfection of humanity.

SAMUEL JOHNSON

❖

Even a child is known by his actions, by whether

his conduct is pure and right.

PROVERBS 20:11

❖

It takes a wise father to know when to push his son out of the nest. It's painful, but it has to be done. I'll always be thankful that my dad gave me wings and then made me use them. ❖

MAX LUCADO

Men are never manlier than when they are tender

with their children . . . whether holding a baby in

their arms, loving their grade-schooler, or hugging

their teenager or adult children.

R. KENT HUGHES

❖

Great is the Lord and most worthy of praise;

his greatness no one can fathom. One generation

will commend your works to another; they will

tell of your mighty acts. ◆

PSALM 145:3-4

I like to remind myself, as a parent, that God holds

me responsible to, not for, my children!

LEE EZELL

And what does the LORD require of you?

To act justly and to love mercy and to

walk humbly with your God.

MICAH 6:8B

❖

The minutes you invest in prayer and God's
Word won't return void. They will cultivate your
spiritual life and carve out a legacy of love
in your child's life as well.

JOHN TRENT

❖

He who fears the LORD has a secure fortress,

and for his children it will be a refuge.

PROVERBS 14 : 26

❖

The thing that has saved the day for me with my children, and also with my wife, is to be transparent and to admit I'm not perfect. Instead of covering over mistakes, I own up to them. Then the way is cleared for forgiveness. ❖

DR. KEVIN LEMAN

Often we fathers are called upon not only to choose

between our children and our work, but between

convenience and the inconvenience

of keeping a promise.

TONY EVANS

❖

What the Church needs today is not more machinery or better, not new organizations or more and novel methods, but men whom the Holy Ghost can use—men of prayer, men mighty in prayer.

EDWARD M. BOUNDS

❖

Only the Lord knows how many children lose heart because their fathers have hard days. ◆

R. KENT HUGHES

Discipline your son, and he will give you peace;

he will bring delight to your soul.

PROVERBS 29:17

Don't allow the mundane or the frantic to rob you

of a joyful family life. Don't let the hope of "someday"

distract you from the blessings of today.

KURT   BRUNER

❖

If children are going to be free to enjoy their
childhood and develop at their God-given pace,
we must abandon the notion that they
should be pushed to outshine their peers.
In some cases, a well-meaning push to
succeed . . . squeezes the precious gift
of innocence out of them.

DOUG FIELDS

❖

It does no good to insist that your child's tone of

voice and actions reflect honor toward you if

you don't show them how it's done.

G A R Y   S M A L L E Y

❖

From everlasting to everlasting the LORD's love is with those who fear him, and his righteousness with their children's children. ❖

PSALM 103:17

You have to instruct children in the things of the Lord if they are going to do what's right. ◆

TONY EVANS

Parents, never underestimate

the importance of your presence.

ANONYMOUS

Discipline without love breeds resentment.

Discipline with love builds character.

GARY CHAPMAN

❖

Wise parents will talk about God throughout

the day and talk with him in the presence

of their children.

JOHN DETTONI

❖

Tell it to your children, and let your children

tell it to their children, and their children

to the next generation.

JOEL 1:3

❖

Children are not . . . born to fulfill their parents' frustrated dreams. Each child has his or her own special place to fill. ❖

MARCIA L. MITCHELL

Character is what you are in the dark.

DWIGHT L. MOODY

❖

To be genuinely concerned about the interests of others, you must be genuinely committed to the interests of Christ.

JOSEPH STOWELL

❖

The most profound way I let my family know

I love them is by giving them time.

ADRIAN ROGERS

❖

Commitment means responsibility, and responsibility sounds confining. For example, it is common in our day to define freedom as the complete absence of restraint. . . . Absolute freedom is absolute nonsense! We gain freedom in anything through commitment, discipline, and fixed habit. ◆

RICHARD J. FOSTER

Parents know that children rank the words "not yet"

as nearly the most awful in the English language,

second only to the word "no."

BILL HYBELS

Be completely humble and gentle; be patient,

bearing with one another in love.

EPHESIANS 4:2

Our kids are like two-legged mirrors, reflecting a lot of what is inside us. Sometimes the reflection is amusing, sometimes it's affirming, other times it's alarming. When parents look at their children, they ultimately find they are also looking at themselves. ❖

RON HUTCHCRAFT

A mirror reflects a man's face, but what he is really

like is shown by the kinds of friends he chooses.

PROVERBS 27:19 (TLB)

❖

The Church in America needs real men,

and we are the men.

R. KENT HUGHES

❖

It is easy to tell a lie but hard to tell only one.

SISSELA BOK

❖

Discipline your son, for in that there is hope. . . .

❖

To call a child "stupid" reveals more about our own

intelligence than it does about the child's.

GARY CHAPMAN

❖

Integrity is what you do when

no one is looking.

ANONYMOUS

137

When a dad imparts a code of conduct, when he

establishes boundaries and reinforces truth,

a son is forever strengthened.

ROBERT LEWIS

❖

You cannot have children who will honor

you and obey God if you don't want to

invest time and energy in them.

TONY EVANS

❖

Do not become so obsessed by reading books on how to be a parent that you don't have time left over to actually parent. ◆

GARY CHAPMAN

The fear of the LORD teaches a man wisdom,

and humility comes before honor.

PROVERBS 15:33

Dad can encourage his child profoundly by

taking part in the child's hobbies.

FRANK MINIRTH

The more Dad and Mom love each other, the more secure their children will feel. ❖

JAY STRACK

I believe in Christ like I believe in the sun, not just because I see it, but because by it I can see everything else. ◆

C.S. LEWIS

How great is the love the Father has lavished on us,

that we should be called the children of God!

And that is what we are!

1 JOHN 3:1A

❖

Fear of God builds churches, but love of God builds men.

LOUIS O. WILLIAMS

❖

All growth that is not towards God

is growing to decay.

GEORGE MACDONALD

❖

Christianity is the good man's text;

his life, the illustration.

JOSEPH P. THOMPSON

❖

A patient man has great understanding, but a quick-tempered man displays folly. ❖

PROVERBS 14:29

Encouraging words motivate positive behavior;

condemning words stifle effort.

GARY CHAPMAN

Prayer is the signature of the soul on the

correspondence with our Creator.

C O R R I E   T E N   B O O M

❖

A commitment to marriage is the first step

to building a strong family.

ROLF ZETTERSTEN

❖

Train a child in the way he should go, and when he is old he will not turn from it. ◆

PROVERBS 22:6

What do your children see you playing, polishing, mowing, or pruning with gusto? Do they ever get that much time and attention from you? For the roots of honor to sink deeply, your children must feel that they are at least as valuable as your work, hobbies, leisure pursuits, and possessions.

GARY SMALLEY

❖

When delivering praise and criticism, never for a

moment believe that your child understands your

true feelings. You have to express them. Nicely.

FRANK MINIRTH

In teaching our children to honor us, we are teaching them ultimately to honor God.

TONY EVANS

❖

You need to persevere so that when you

have done the will of God, you will

receive what he has promised.

HEBREWS 10:36

❖